It's Not Just a PARACHUTE

INTEGRATIVE ACTIVITIES FOR CHILDREN OF ALL ABILITIES

by Mary L. Witoski, B.P.E., B.Sc.(OT)

Therapy Skill Builders
A division of
Communication Skill Builders
3830 E. Bellevue/P.O. Box 42050
Tucson, Arizona 85733/(602) 323-7500

Published and distributed by

Therapy Skill Builders
A division of
Communication Skill Builders
3830 E. Bellevue/P.O. Box 42050
Tucson, Arizona 85733/(602) 323-7500

© 1992 by Mary L. Witoski

All rights reserved. No parts of this book may be reproduced or transmitted in any form or by any means, electronic or mechanical, including photocopying and recording, or by any information storage and retrieval system, without written permission from the Publisher.

ISBN 0-88450-480-8   Catalog No. 4733

10 9 8 7 6 5 4 3 2 1
Printed in the United States of America

This book was developed under a grant from the Canadian Occupational Therapy Foundation.

About the Author

Mary Louise Witoski, B.P.E. (University of New Brunswick), B.Sc.(OT) (Dalhousie University), has experience working with children whose difficulties include emotional and developmental disabilities, physical disabilities, learning disabilities, and sensory integration dysfunctions. Her background in sports science/administration and adapted physical education and her present work in pediatric occupational therapy provide a unique interdisciplinary understanding of program development. In 1988 she was honored with the Award of Excellence from the Association for Media and Technology in Canada.

Dedication

In memory of my mother,
who dedicated her life to helping others.

Acknowledgments

I would like to thank friends and family
for their support and encouragement.

A special thanks to
David Batstone, Dorothy Skinner,
Marnie Crow, Diane Watson, Sylvia Wilson,
Nikki Kahl, and Judith Tharp
for their welcomed support.

Contents

Introduction 1

About the Parachute 2
    Developmental Benefits 2
    Unique Characteristics of the Parachute 4
    How to Make Your Own Parachute 6
    Care of the Parachute 8
    Where to Use the Parachute 8
    Group Size for Parachute Activities 9
    Steps to Promote Integrative Parachute Activities . 9
    How to Use the Parachute 10

Parachute Activities 12
    Guide Sheet 12
    Waves 13
    Exchange 14
    Follow the Leader 16
    Blanket Touch 17
    Sing-a-Long 18
    Statues 23
    Roll-Up 24
    Hot Dog 26
    Monsters 26
    Merry-Go-Round 27
    Jaws 28
    Parachute Throw 29
    Magic Carpet 30
    Empty the Parachute 31
    Ball Roll 32
    Mountain 33
    Spaceship 35

Appendix: Common Childhood Conditions 37

References 48

Additional Sources 48

Introduction

Children of all ages and on many levels of physical, social, cognitive, and communicative abilities enjoy playing with parachutes. It is very motivating and brings a special sense of togetherness to the participants.

This book will help to illustrate the parachute's unique properties and developmental benefits. Its goals are to help you discover the integrative value of the parachute and explore creative activities for children with and without special needs.

This book is intended for use by people of many different backgrounds including health, education, and recreation professionals and nonprofessionals. Although the book focuses on children, the content is easily applied to other age groups and abilities.

About the Parachute

Developmental Benefits

Play

Play, the process of experiencing, exploring, and manipulating past with current and future experiences, is a natural means of exploring the environment. It is a developmental process which contributes to overall physical, cognitive, and social development.

As a "play thing," the parachute is very exciting and appealing. It piques a child's curiosity as to how it works. It can be manipulated easily, and it responds immediately to every action. These factors are important if a "play thing" is to be used again and again.

Physical Benefits

A moving parachute creates a force of resistance as it traps air underneath. When the children lower the parachute, resistance develops as the air is compressed. In turn, when the parachute is raised, air underneath is released, and resistance develops as the parachute pushes air upward.

In addition to promoting general muscular strength, many parachute activities foster cardiovascular fitness from walking, running, pushing, or wheeling a wheelchair. Remember, for an activity to have a cardiovascular benefit, the activity should be repeated a minimum of three times a week for at least 15 minutes, at a moderate level of intensity. Physical demands can be modified by changing the size of the parachute; having children lying, sitting, or standing; or altering the speed at which the parachute is moved.

Many parachute activities also focus on general body coordination. Children coordinate their body movements to manipulate the parachute for a given response. Many activities include balls, sponges, balloons, and other objects to promote eye-hand coordination. For instance, the goal of an activity might be to move a ball around the perimeter of the parachute without letting it fall off the outer edge or disappear through the hole in the center of the parachute. In this case, children must track the path of the ball, being careful not to raise the parachute too high or too low.

Learning Benefits

Parachute activities promote many skills involved in the learning process, particularly the primary skills of listening and following directions. Children want to listen, perhaps, because the end result is a powerful reinforcer. You can delay the end result by expanding the number of sequences to be completed. Instructions can be simple or complex, and can be given with or without verbal or visual cues.

You can also promote other aspects of cognition and perception, including development of concepts (colors, numbers, shape, size), directionality (in, out, over, under, through, on, off), laterality (left, right), and spatial relationships (depth perception, figure-ground).

Language

Listening skills and the ability to follow directions are not only important to cognitive skills, they are also essential components of functional communication. Turn taking is another important communication skill, and most parachute activities provide opportunities to practice this. To play "Exchange," for example, half of the children must hold onto the parachute, lifting it up over their heads so the other children can move underneath to the opposite side.

The parachute also offers many opportunities to incorporate the development of receptive and expressive language skills. Many different action verbs can be used in parachute activities. Using action verbs enhances not only the child's receptive and expressive language skills but also the expression of movement. Listed below are some action verbs that can be used in the context of parachute activities.

Action Words for Parachute Activities

accelerating	bouncing	clapping	dipping	flexing	jumping
arching	boxing	climbing	diving	fluttering	kicking
ascending	bucking	collapsing	dragging	following	knocking
attaching	building	connecting	dropping	galloping	leading
attacking	bumping	copying	escaping	giggling	leaping
balancing	carrying	covering	expanding	growing	lifting
batting	catching	crashing	exploding	hopping	limping
bending	chasing	crawling	exploring	hunting	lowering
blowing	cheering	creeping	falling	itching	lurching
bobbing	chopping	dancing	feeling	jogging	mopping
bolting	chugging	digging	flapping	juggling	moving

nodding	riding	shifting	squeezing	swooping	unwinding
panting	rising	sinking	stacking	tagging	vibrating
passing	rocking	skidding	stamping	tapping	waving
pivoting	rolling	skipping	steering	throwing	weaving
pouncing	rowing	sliding	stepping	thumping	whispering
puffing	running	snapping	stooping	tickling	whistling
pulling	sailing	snuggling	straddling	touching	wiggling
pumping	scampering	soaring	strolling	trotting	winding
punching	scooting	spinning	strutting	tugging	zigzagging
pushing	scrubbing	splashing	swaying	twirling	zooming
racing	shaking	springing	swimming	twisting	
reaching	shaving	squatting	swinging	tying	

Social

Parachute activities are motivating and promote a sense of belonging and togetherness. Because of their cooperative nature, parachute activities de-emphasize individual differences. Children at many levels of physical, cognitive, and communicative abilities can enjoy positive social interactions. For example, a child who cannot hold onto the parachute can signal to the others when to let go of the parachute. The child can sit with the others around the parachute and will be able to contribute to the game.

Parachute activities also can be used to explore feelings and emotions. The children can move the parachute to express joy, anger, sadness, and so on.

Unique Characteristics of the Parachute

It does not take long to discover the unique aspects of the parachute. Among these special qualities are the ways it appeals to our senses of touch, sight, and—surprisingly—temperature.

Touch

The nylon of the parachute is very smooth and soft to touch. Draping the parachute over body parts or layering it upon itself creates an airy feeling of weightlessness. When the parachute is lowered, the air underneath is compressed. Then, when it is raised, the air is released and a light breeze escapes from underneath. Depending on the number of children participating, the size of the parachute, and the intensity with which the parachute is worked, the released air pressure can range from a light to a strong breeze.

Children enjoy lying, sitting, crawling, and walking on or under the parachute. However, during parachute activities, most of the tactile feedback is incidental. Children often appear to be more concerned about playing the game than paying attention to the tactile stimulation. For those who are bothered by the sensation, adjust the amount of contact to suit individual levels of tolerance.

(List of action words adapted from Kuntzleman et al. 1982, pp. 317-318)

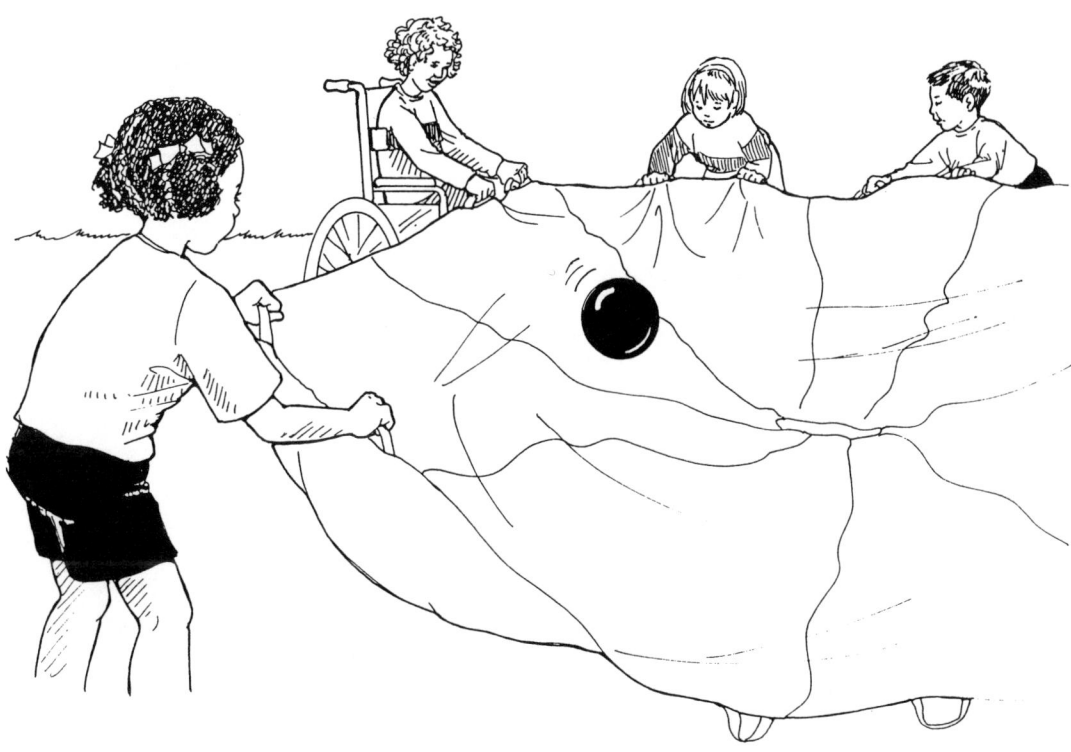

Visual

The color combinations of the parachute add to the visual appeal. (The instructions in the section on "How to Make Your Own Parachute" allow you to create your own color combinations.)

During parachute activities, the parachute can be quickly transformed from one- to three-dimensional shapes and back again. This gives children a delightful sense of control and ability to effect change. The open hole in the center of the parachute not only adds visual appeal but also allows objects such as balls and balloons to be dropped through the hole. Some children can sit or lie underneath the open hole while the rest of the children move the parachute up and down above them.

Powerful visual images are created when the parachute is used outdoors, especially on a bright sunny day. The sun shines onto the parachute, lighting up the colors, forming a dark shadow underneath, and sending a solid beam of light through the hole in the center. Indoors, you can create different shadow effects by adjusting the light source in the activity area (dimming lights, pulling down window blinds, placing dark fabric below the light source).

Temperature

The nylon fabric of the parachute feels cool and silky against the skin. In addition, because of its synthetic composition, nylon does not "breathe" as readily as natural fibers. During enclosed activities (such as "Spaceship"), the parachute's fabric traps the body heat generated by those sitting under the parachute, markedly raising the temperature within the closed-in space. When children come out from under a parachute where they have been enclosed for a while, they will notice that the room-temperature air feels cooler than the inside of the "spaceship."

How to Make Your Own Parachute

If you want to have different sizes or colors of parachutes, you can make your own by sewing together triangle-shaped panels of light-weight nylon. The steps are described below.

First, decide on the overall diameter of the parachute. Estimate the number of children in your group and select the appropriate diameter. (See the section on "Group Size for Parachute Activities" for some helpful guidelines.) The easiest way to visualize the size is to draw or tape a circle on the floor.

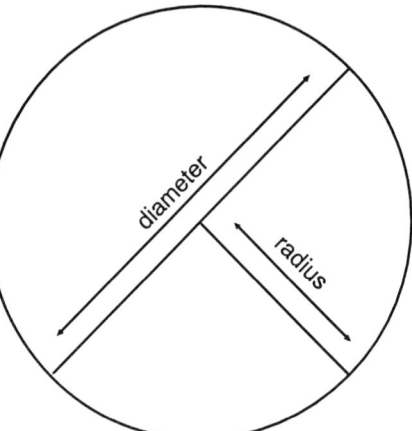

Mark the approximate center of the circle you have laid out on the floor and measure the radius of the parachute. This will be the length of the triangle seams from the center to the outside edge. The diameter of your parachute will be twice this figure.

Decide how many panels you want in the parachute. For smaller parachutes, eight panels are appropriate; larger parachutes will need more panels. To find out the minimum number of panels you will need, determine the circumference of your parachute for the diameter you have chosen (convert the diameter measurement to inches and multiply by *pi*, 3.14). Then divide that circumference measurement by the width of the nylon you will use. (Most light-weight and ripstop nylon available in fabric stores is 45 or 60 inches wide.) For example, if you want to make a 10-foot parachute, convert the 10-foot diameter to inches:

10 feet x 12 inches/foot = 120 inches

Then determine the circumference:

120 inches x 3.14 (pi) = 377 inches

Now, divide the circumference (377 inches) by the width of the fabric you will use, and round the answer off to the next highest number. In the example below, a fabric width of 45 inches is used:

377 inches ÷ 45-inch fabric = 8.37 panels

Round off 8.37 to the next highest number, 9. You will need a minimum of nine panels to make a flat, 10-foot parachute.

If, in order to create a specific visual effect, you want to use more than the minimum number of panels determined above, you will need to divide the circumference by the number of panels you want to use. This will give you the width of the base of each triangle panel. For example, if you want a 10-foot parachute to have 12 panels instead of the minimum number of 9, divide the circumference (377 inches) by 12 panels:

377 inches ÷ 12 panels = 31.4 inches

Each triangle will measure 5 feet along the side and approximately 31.5 inches in width at the base. Add one-half inch to this measurement, to give a one-quarter-inch seam allowance down each side. (Make sure the width you come up with does not exceed the width of the fabric you will use, or you will have to piece the panels.)

To determine the amount of fabric you need to purchase, decide on how many panels of each color you want. You can cut two panels from one piece of fabric the length of the parachute's radius: one triangle panel ("Triangle A" in Figure 1 below) will be cut in one piece, out of the middle of the fabric.

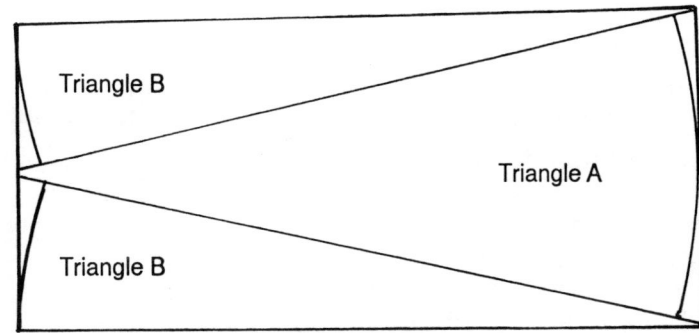

Figure 1

The other panel will be sewn together (with a one-quarter-inch seam allowance) from the two triangles ("B" in Figure 1) left along the sides after you cut the first panel.

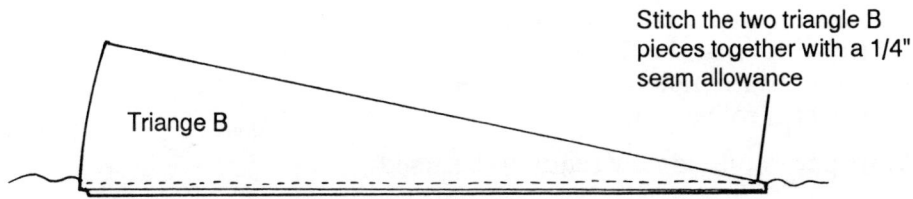

After you have cut all the panels, it is a good idea to sear the edges of the nylon to prevent them from fraying with the heavy use the parachute will receive. Hold the edge of the parachute taut between your two hands and run the raw edge of the nylon quickly through a candle flame, being careful that any frayed threads do not catch fire and burn into the fabric. (You can pinch out any burning fibers; the flame is not very hot.) Be sure there is adequate ventilation.

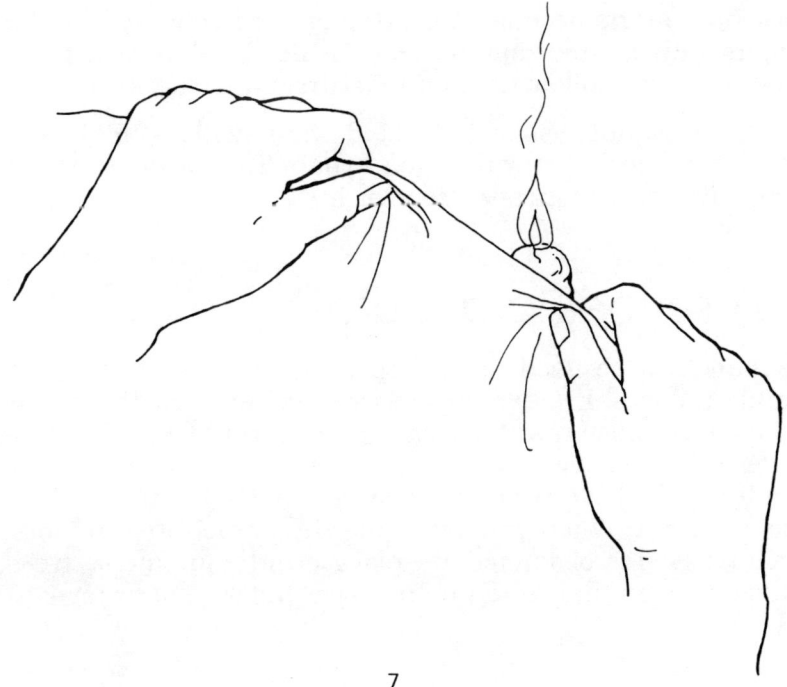

Pin the triangle panels together in the desired color sequence, and sew the long edges together. Use good-quality thread and reinforce the seams by double-stitching or using a reinforced overlock stitch.

Trim the outer edge of the parachute, if necessary, to correct the shaping. Sear any newly cut edges. Finish the outer edge of the parachute with a narrow hem. You can put handles around the outer edge for the children to hold onto. Cut nylon webbing into 6- to 8-inch lengths, allowing two handles per panel. Sear the ends of the webbing with a candle flame to prevent raveling. Space the handles evenly around the parachute and sew them on securely.

Decide if you want to put a hole in the center of the parachute. A hole allows the entrapped air to escape, and there are a variety of exciting activities that can be done only with this type of parachute. If you want to make a hole, fold the parachute in quarters or eighths (see Figure 2) and cut out the center of the parachute in an arc with a radius of 5 inches. Unfold the parachute and see if this size hole is adequate. If not, refold the parachute and cut out a little more. Sear the cut fabric with a candle flame, and finish the edge of the hole with an overlock serger or a rolled hem.

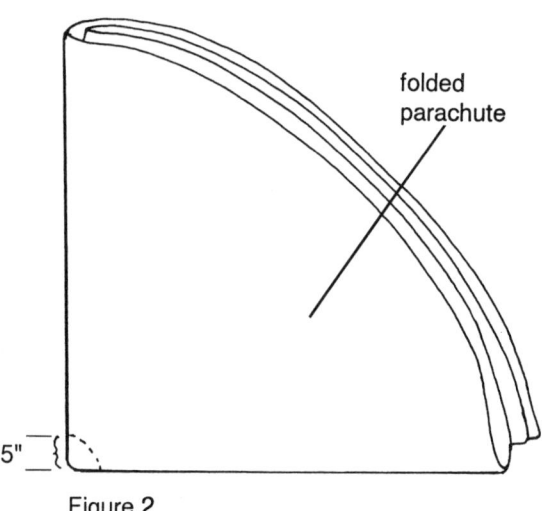

Figure 2

Your parachute is now ready to be used.

Care of the Parachute

The parachute requires minimum storage space and maintenance. To contain the slippery fabric and to keep it from becoming torn or soiled during storage and removal, store the parachute in a nylon or mesh bag. The parachute and bag should be stored in an area that stays near room temperature.

If the parachute fabric becomes torn, repair it as soon as possible. You can make repairs with ripstop tape or seam sealer, sold as tent-repair items in most camping stores; follow the manufacturer's instructions.

To clean the parachute, soak it in cold water with a mild detergent. For stubborn stains, scrub dirt with a soft brush. To dry, lay the parachute out flat, or drape it over a suspended rope or line.

Where to Use the Parachute

The parachute can be used in any open space, free of obstructions, both indoors and outdoors. Enough space is needed to allow the parachute to be opened to its full diameter, with a clearance of 8 to 10 feet behind the children. It is also desirable to have enough height clearance to allow the parachute to drift when it is raised overhead and released. A 15- to 20-foot-high clearance should be sufficient. When you are using the parachute outdoors, choose a level area that is free of immediate playground equipment, trees, or other obstructions, to keep the parachute from getting caught or torn.

Another consideration when using the parachute outdoors is the direction and speed of wind currents. If the wind gusts are too strong, children may have difficulty controlling the parachute. However, a light breeze aids in the fullness of shapes as the parachute is manipulated.

Group Size for Parachute Activities

Generally, the larger the parachute, the more children needed to work it. Although any number of children and group leaders or assistants can work a parachute, it may be more strenuous with too few participants, and some activities may be more difficult to perform. The following guidelines will help you decide the number of children for different parachute sizes.

Parachute Diameter	Number of Children
6 feet	5 to 10
15 feet	10 to 20
21 feet	15 or more
32 feet	20 or more

For children under 5 years of age, a medium- or small-sized parachute is recommended. Children over 5 years of age generally can manage a medium or large size.

If you find your parachute is too large, you can reduce its overall diameter by having the children roll the outside edges in toward the center. (This also gives the children a larger roll of fabric to grasp). Attach velcro straps to hold down the folded-in edges securely. You can also reduce the parachute's overall diameter by cutting off a few inches around the outside and rehemming it.

Steps to Promote Integrative Parachute Activities

Before you begin parachute activities, determine if any of the participating children have special needs. Talk to the primary caregivers for special instructions. (Consult the Appendix on "Common Childhood Conditions" if you need a brief description of a child's condition or a source for further information.) Always try to choose parachute activities that are not only age-appropriate but within the skill levels of the children. You may also wish to alter the complexity of an activity by modifying the number of steps and/or the time required to complete the activity.

Try to adjust the sensory aspects of vision and hearing to best meet the children's needs. When playing indoors, for example, you can brighten or dim the light source with dimmers or turn lights on or off. You can enhance the visual and tactile appeal of parachute activities by attaching brightly colored objects (plastic or felt letters, animals, shapes) to the parachute. You can use fluorescent tape or paint to make a circle on the floor or put directions on the wall to help visually impaired children see directions. Taped music, action songs, and musical instruments (drum, tambourine, rhythm sticks) can enhance the integrative value of parachute activities.

Different-sized objects such as balls or balloons can alter the integrative value. Increasing the size of the object promotes visual identification and tracking.

(If increased size is needed but a larger object is too heavy, try objects made of lightweight materials such as plastic or sponge.) Decreasing the size of the object promotes visual discrimination. If you decrease the size of the object, however, you may need to increase the weight to ensure control.

If a child uses a wheelchair, remember that it is a means of mobility and may not be the only option for mobility or seating. To enhance the child's integration in as many parachute activities as possible, explore with primary caregivers and professionals (physical or occupational therapists) other means of mobility and supported sitting positions. Alternatives need to be safe, comfortable, and functional.

In a group setting, a ratio of 50:50 (children with and without special needs) may not be ideal. Ratios of 40:60 or 30:70 may promote modelling of normalcy and remove the chances of separate groups, thus promoting social integration.

When children need assistance to participate in an activity, it is best to let them pick their own buddies. For parachute activities requiring the child to be lifted and carried, the buddy may need to be an adult. Depending on the activity, the buddy may be positioned beside, behind, or across from the child.

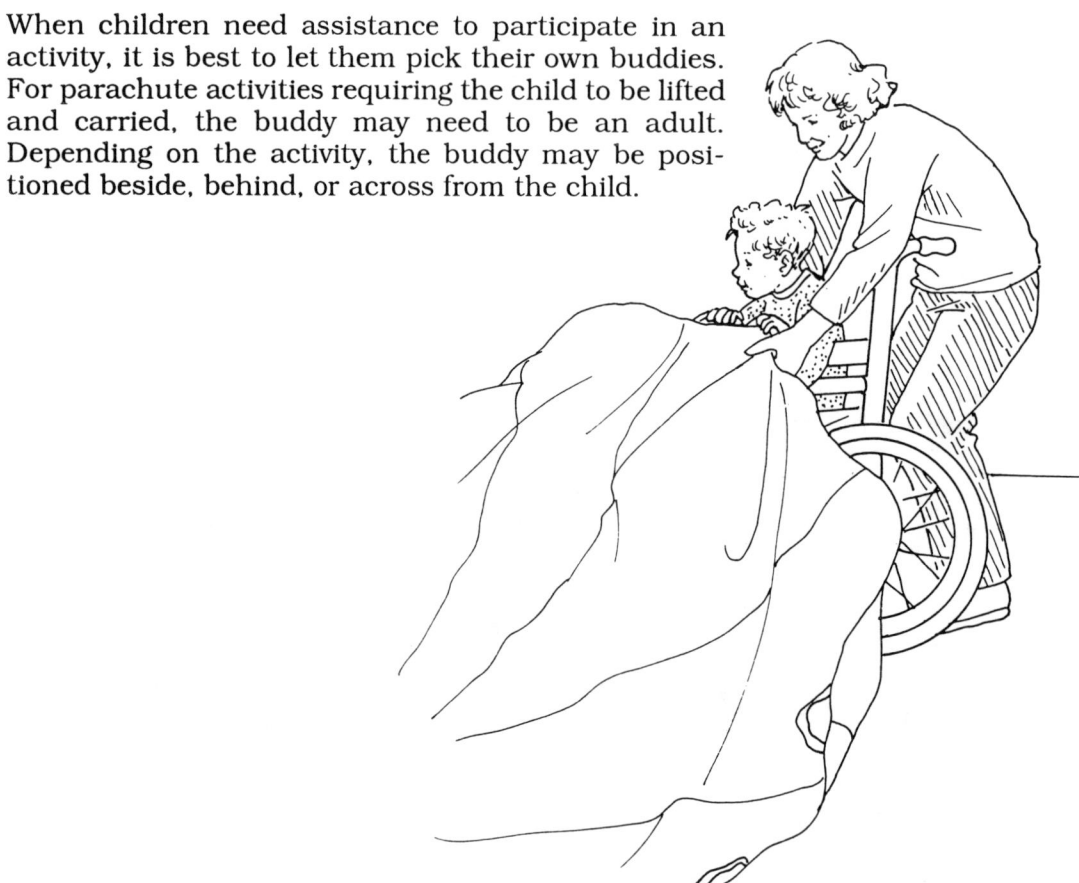

How to Use the Parachute

To introduce parachute activities to a group of children, have them sit down in a circle with you in the center. Keep the parachute in its bag as you review two important rules: (1) children are not to run and jump on or go under the parachute unless that action is part of the activity, and (2) children are not to let go of the parachute unless that action is part of the activity.

The next step is to select one or two children to help you pull the parachute out of its bag and spread it out on the floor. Next, ask the children to space themselves around the outside of the parachute. To space the children evenly, you can assign children to different color panels of the parachute.

Have everyone stand up and grasp the edge of the parachute. Children can get a better hold on the parachute if they roll up the edges two or three times. (This may be unnecessary if your parachute has handles.) The children may automatically start to move the parachute up and down. At this point, show the children how to work the parachute. For most activities, it is important that the children move the parachute up and down together. Depending on the age of the children, you may simply model the activities, and the children will pick up the rhythm. You can also use specific counting methods to more closely direct the movement: "one-parachute, two-parachute . . ." or "one, two, three." Regardless of the method you use to direct the rhythm of the activity, always begin with a signal such as, "Get set, go."

Now you are ready to start any of the suggested parachute activities. Some of the activities have been collected from cited references; however, all contain original ideas created from practical experiences. The descriptions are intended as suggestions only, and as time goes by you will discover many more activities that you or the children will make up.

Parachute Activities

For convenience, the parachute activities have been arranged progressively from easy (introductory) to more difficult (advanced cooperative). The guide below notes the different skills promoted by each activity. You can use this information in planning specific goal-directed activities. Keep in mind, however, that the parachute's primary use is as a play medium. It is important, above all, to have fun.

GUIDE SHEET

Learning Benefits	Introductory Activities					Intermediate Imaginative Activities						Advanced Cooperative Activities					
	Waves	Exchange	Follow the Leader	Blanket Touch	Sing-a-Long	Statues	Roll-Up	Hot Dog	Monsters	Merry-Go-Round	Jaws	Parachute Throw	Magic Carpet	Empty the Parachute	Ball Roll	Mountain	Spaceship
Physical Skills																	
Basic Motor Patterns	•	•	•	•	•	•	•	•	•	•	•	•	•	•	•	•	•
Strength	•					•				•		•	•	•	•	•	•
Endurance		•								•		•	•	•	•	•	•
Coordination	•	•	•	•	•	•	•			•		•	•	•	•	•	•
Ball Skills	•	•												•	•	•	•
Social Skills																	
Listening	•	•	•	•	•	•	•	•	•	•	•	•	•	•	•	•	•
Turn Taking		•	•	•	•	•	•	•	•	•	•	•	•	•	•	•	•
Cooperation	•	•	•	•	•	•	•	•	•	•	•	•	•	•	•	•	•
Trust				•			•	•		•			•			•	•
Relaxation	•	•		•		•	•					•	•			•	•
Language Skills																	
Receptive	•	•	•		•	•		•	•	•	•	•		•	•		•
Expressive	•	•	•	•	•	•	•	•	•	•	•	•	•	•	•	•	•
Sequencing	•	•	•	•	•	•	•	•	•	•	•	•	•	•	•	•	•
Sensory Systems																	
Tactile	•	•	•	•	•	•	•	•	•	•	•	•	•	•	•	•	•
Visual	•	•	•	•	•	•	•	•	•	•	•	•	•	•	•	•	•
Auditory	•		•	•	•					•				•	•	•	•
Cognitive Skills																	
Directionality		•	•		•	•	•	•	•	•	•		•	•	•		•
Size Concepts	•	•		•		•	•	•	•			•	•	•	•	•	•
Object and Shape Concepts				•		•	•	•				•	•	•	•	•	•
Quantities			•	•	•	•						•		•	•	•	•
Attention	•	•	•	•	•	•	•	•	•	•	•	•	•	•	•	•	•
Body Schema			•	•	•	•	•	•	•		•		•			•	•
Same and Different		•				•							•	•	•	•	•

Waves

Spread the parachute out fully and space the children evenly around the outside. The children can play this activity sitting, kneeling, or standing around the outside of the parachute. Have the children hold onto the edge of the parachute and lift it up and move it down. Try varying the speed at which the parachute is moved up and down and the height to which it is raised.

Adaptations

Place small balls on top of the parachute. While the children make waves, they try to keep the balls from falling off.

Have some of the children try crawling, walking, or wheeling wheelchairs over the top of the parachute while the rest of the children hold onto the parachute and make waves.

Lower the parachute to the floor and have all of the children sit or kneel around the outside. Ask a few children to lie on top of the parachute. They can lie still or pretend they are swimming (imitating different strokes—dog paddle, back-crawl). The rest of the children continue to hold onto the parachute and make waves.

Some children may wish to try going underneath the parachute. Divide the group in half and have one half of the children go underneath while the rest of the children hold onto the parachute and make waves. If a child needs physical assistance to get under the parachute, ask the children making waves to lift the parachute up high enough so the child can be positioned safely. The helper may need to stay with the child if the child is timid or needs additional physical support.

Exchange

Spread the parachute out fully and space the children evenly around the outside. It is best to play this activity with the children standing (with or without support) or remaining seated in their wheelchairs. The children lift the parachute up over their heads so they can see each other beneath the parachute. The higher they are able to lift the parachute, the more room there will be underneath for children to see where to move. While the parachute is up in the air, call out a child's name. That child quickly moves under the parachute across to the other side.

Adaptations

Divide the children into groups (animals, colors of the parachute, boys/girls). Once the parachute is lifted up, call out categories (for example, "All the yellows exchange"). The children in that group quickly proceed under the parachute across to the opposite side. If you use different animals for the group designations, the children can imitate that animal's walk and sounds.

As a child is moving under the parachute to the other side, the rest of the children slowly lower the parachute to the floor. The child making the exchange tries to get to the other side before being touched by the parachute.

As the children lift the parachute, call out a child's name. That child lets go of the parachute and quickly proceeds around the outside of the parachute, returning to the original spot. You can call two children at the same time. For younger children, the direction they proceed around the parachute may not matter. For older children, you can specify "left" or "right" to designate a clockwise or counterclockwise direction.

Place a ball or other object on the floor under the parachute. Call out a child's name. All the children lift up the parachute. Once the parachute has been lifted up, the designated child lets go of the parachute, quickly moves under the parachute to pick up the object, and then returns to the original spot. You may wish to call two children at the same time and see who can retrieve the object first. You can make this activity less competitive by placing two objects on the floor, one for each child.

Have the children hold onto the parachute while you let go and walk around the parachute, whispering to each child a different animal name. The children begin to move the parachute up and down. After three up-and-down repetitions, call out an animal name. Those children called move under the parachute, imitating that animal. The rest of the children try to guess what animal is being imitated. Animals that are fun to imitate include bears, birds, bunnies, dogs, ducks, crabs, horses, elephants, snakes, horses, kangaroos, monkeys, seals, and cats.

Follow the Leader

Spread the parachute out fully and space the children evenly around the outside. The children can play this activity sitting, kneeling, or standing around the outside of the parachute.

The children listen and watch you for directions, then they respond with the appropriate action. You can vary the difficulty of your direction by giving more or fewer verbal or visual cues (including verbal instruction accompanied by visual demonstration, visual demonstration without verbal instruction, or verbal instruction without visual demonstration). When you provide fewer cues, the children need to pay attention more closely. Choose the style best suited for the individual needs of the children.

Adaptations

Select and start playing a piece of music. (A tape recorder or record player works best, although someone can beat a rhythm on a drum or you can sing a song as a group.) While the music is playing, the children hold onto the parachute and make "waves" to the music. When you stop the music, the children are to "freeze." The idea is to see how long it takes for everyone to realize the music has stopped. When all the children have stopped, start the music and play the game over again. After the children are familiar with the game, let them take turns stopping the music.

Play the game "Simon Says," the children moving the parachute up or down to designated body parts. (For example, after you say, "Simon says, 'Touch your toes,'" the children lower the parachute down to their toes.)

Blanket Touch

Spread the parachute out fully and space the children evenly around the outside. Have all of the children hold onto the parachute and lift it up. Ask one or two children to lie down on the floor underneath the parachute (on their backs, stomachs, or sides). The rest of the children hold onto the parachute and slowly lift it up and down, barely touching the children underneath. After three or four up-and-down repetitions, ask the children to lower the parachute slowly, covering the children underneath.

As the parachute is lifted and lowered, air is released and a light breeze escapes from underneath to the outside. In this activity, the children underneath the parachute not only experience the effects of the breeze but also feel the weight of the parachute, like a big blanket covering their bodies.

Adaptations

Have the children under the parachute lie together in pairs or any other number combination.

Have the children beneath the parachute try to make different shapes, letters, or numbers, or imitate different animals with their bodies as the parachute is lowered. After lifting the parachute, the children holding onto the parachute try to guess what has been formed.

Spread the parachute out fully and space the children evenly, lying down on their stomachs, feet pointing to the outside. Have the children hold onto the parachute and try to lift it and lower it.

Sing-a-Long

Pick a song from those given below, or use one of your own favorites. As you sing the song, have the group try to move the parachute up, down, and around to the actions described in the song.

Row, Row, Row Your Boat: This song is best performed with the children sitting around the parachute on the floor. Spread the parachute out and have the children sit with their legs stretched out beneath the parachute, similar to a blanket covering their legs. As the song begins, the children on one side of the parachute pull it up toward their shoulders. The children on the opposite side hold on tight and lean forward as the parachute is pulled down toward their toes. Then they lean back and pull the parachute up to their shoulders while the other children lean forward. Learning to coordinate the body movements with the actions of the parachute may take a little practice.

> Row, row, row your boat
> Gently down the stream.
> Merrily, merrily, merrily, merrily;
> Life is but a dream.

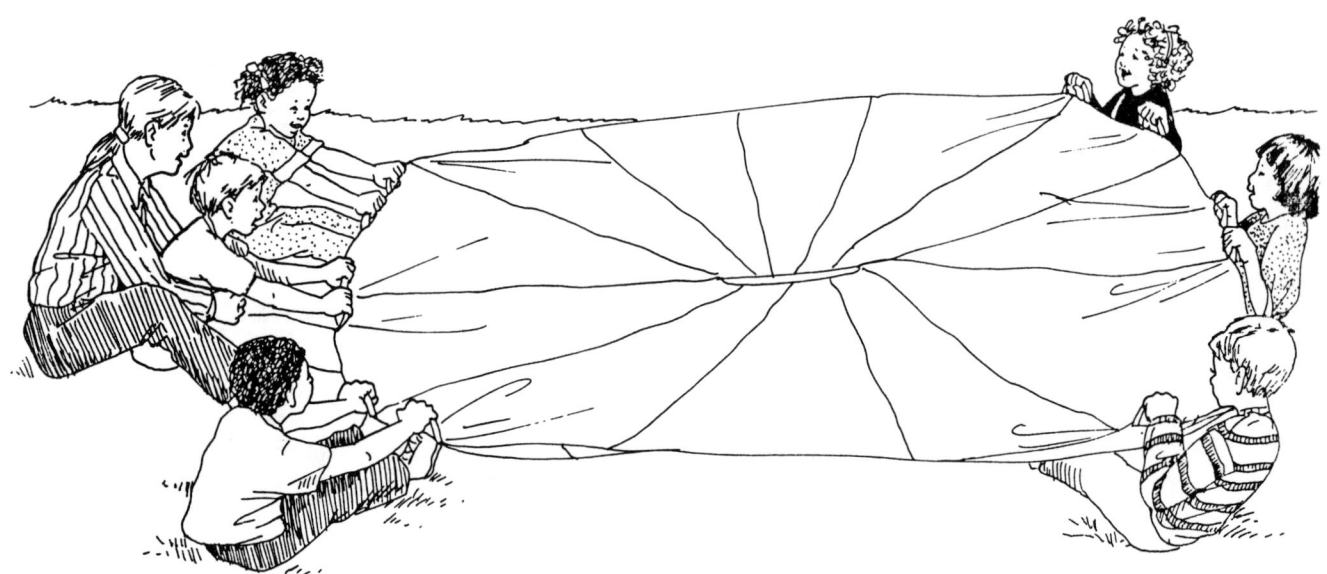

Ring around the Rosie: Spread the parachute out fully and space the children evenly around the outside of the parachute. Have the children hold onto the parachute, turn and face one direction, and walk around in a circle as they sing the song. When you come to the phrase, "we all fall down," the children let go of the parachute and sit down.

> Ring around the rosie,
> A pocket full of posies.
> Husha, husha,
> We all fall down.

Old Red Wagon: Spread the parachute out fully and space the children evenly around the outside. Have the children hold onto the parachute, turn and face one direction, and walk around in a circle as they sing the song. To vary the activity, have one child sit or stand on top of the parachute, in the center, while the rest of the children wind the parachute up around the child, then reverse the direction and unwrap the child.

> Circle to the right, old red wagon.
> Circle to the right, old red wagon.
> Fare thee well, my darling.

Then repeat singing, circling to the left, into the center.

Pop! Goes the Weasel: Spread the parachute out fully and space the children evenly around the outside. Have the children hold onto the parachute, turn and face one direction, and walk around in a circle as they sing the song. When you sing the phrase, "Pop! goes the weasel," everyone jumps, lifting the parachute up high into the air.

>All around the mulberry bush
>The monkey chased the weasel.
>The weasel thought it was all in fun.
>Pop! goes the weasel.

Hokey Pokey: Spread the parachute out fully on the floor and space the children evenly around the outside. This action song can be performed in two ways. For the first option, divide the children into two groups. Half the children will sit or kneel and hold onto the parachute which is resting on the floor. The other children will stand on top of the parachute. The children holding the parachute move it up and down to make waves while the children on top perform the actions in the song.

The other method is to have all the children spaced evenly around the outside of the parachute. As the song is sung, the children make waves in time with the music. When the name of a body part is sung, the children perform the action described. When shaking arms, hands, or legs, have the children hold onto the parachute with one hand for safety.

> You put your right hand in,
> You put your right hand out.
> You put your right hand in, and you shake it all about.
> You do the Hokey Pokey and you turn yourself around;
> That's what it's all about!

Head and Shoulders: Spread the parachute out fully and space the children evenly around the outside. Have the children hold onto the parachute and move it up and down to the body parts named in the song. This song can be performed with the children sitting, standing, kneeling, or even lying on their stomachs or backs on the floor.

> Head, shoulders, knees, and toes,
> Knees and toes, knees and toes.
> Head and shoulders, knees and toes,
> Eyes, ears, mouth, and nose.

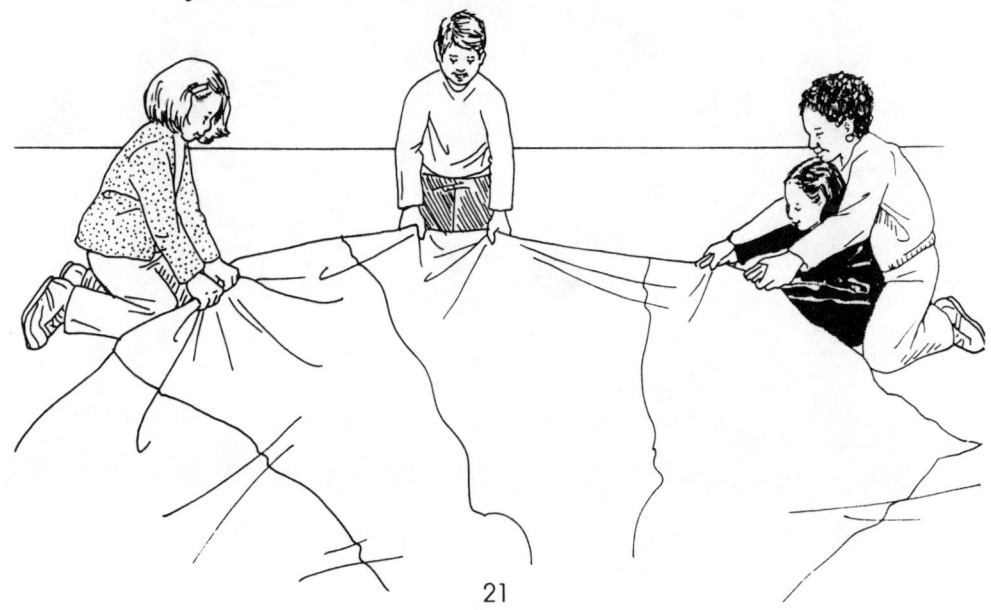

Together: This song also can be performed with the children sitting, kneeling, or standing. As the children sing the song, they can stay in one spot or move into the center of the parachute and back out again.

> The more we get together, together, together,
> The more we get together, the happier we'll be.
> 'Cause your friends are my friends,
> And my friends are your friends.
> The more we get together, the happier we'll be.

Shake Our Sillies Out: Refer to the song "Hokey Pokey" for accompanying parachute actions.

> Well, I gotta shake, shake, shake my sillies out,
> Shake, shake, shake my sillies out,
> And wiggle my waggles away,
> And wiggle my waggles away.
>
> I gotta clap, clap, clap my crazies out.
> I gotta jump, jump, jump my jiggles out.
> I gotta stretch, stretch, stretch my stretches out.
> Hey, I gotta shake, shake, shake my sillies out.

Popcorn: Spread the parachute out fully and space the children evenly around the outside. This song can be performed with the children sitting, kneeling, or standing. Have the children place small balls (pretend "popcorn") on top of the parachute. For the first two phrases of the song, the children move the parachute up and down, being careful not to let the popcorn fall off. When you sing the phrase, "sizzle . . . sizzle pop," lift the parachute up quickly and try to toss the "popcorn balls" off the parachute.

> You put the oil in the pot and you let it get hot.
> You put the popcorn in and start to grin.
> Sizzle sizzle sizzle sizzle pop!

Where is . . . ? This is a good introductory song for welcoming children to the activity, but it can also be used any time during a session. Spread the parachute out fully and space the children evenly around the outside, sitting, kneeling, or standing. Try making small waves up and down as you sing the first two phrases. Then, holding on tight, lift the parachute up high to say, "Hello."

> Where is [child's name]?
> Where is [child's name]?
> There he [she] is, there he [she] is!
> Say hello to [child's name].

Good-Bye: Spread the parachute out fully and space the children evenly around the outside. This song can be performed sitting, kneeling, or standing. This is a song commonly used to end a session. After a child's name is called, that child can be directed to leave the parachute and go to a predetermined waiting area. It is a good idea to group two or three children together when singing this song.

> Bye bye, [first child's name];
> Bye bye, [second child's name];
> Bye bye, [third child's name];
> It's time to say bye bye . . .

Statues

Spread the parachute out fully and space the children evenly around the outside. The children hold onto the parachute and make waves. On the count of three, lift the parachute up high and have two or three children go underneath. Instruct the children beneath the parachute to move around in different ways (crawling, rolling, or pushing or driving wheelchairs). After three wave repetitions, ask the children underneath to freeze like statues while the children on the outside lower the parachute to cover the "statues" underneath. Point out the different shapes and forms created by the parachute-covered children. Call out "Go!" to start the game over again. Let the same group of children underneath the parachute repeat the activity before they resume their places around the outside.

Adaptations

Ask the children underneath the parachute to interpret becoming as tall or small, long or short, wide or thin as possible. The children can express these concepts individually or in small groups.

Keep the parachute covered over the children as they move around being silent, making lots of noise, or imitating different animals.

Roll-Up

Spread the parachute out on the floor and space the children evenly around the outside. As the children stand or kneel, help them fold two sides of the parachute into the center as many times as necessary to reduce the width of the folded parachute to the length of a child's body.

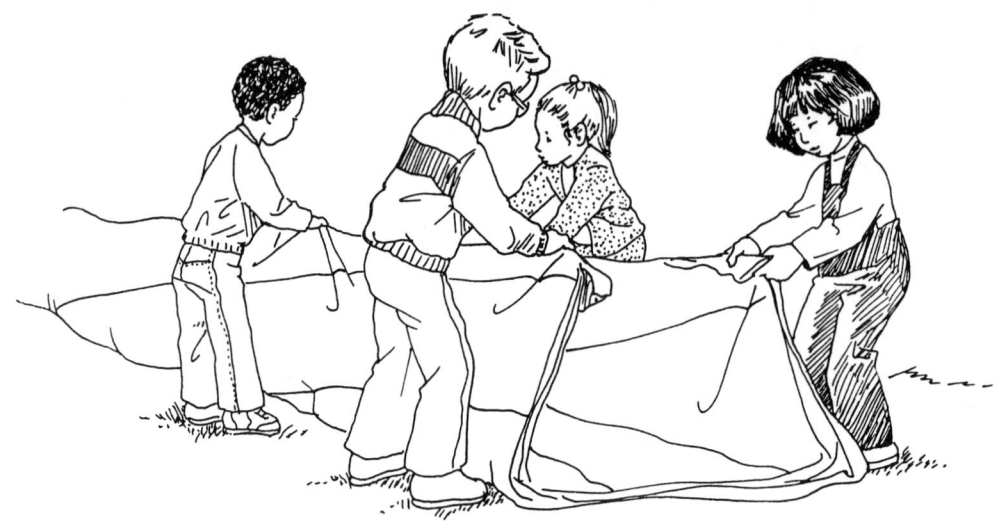

Have a child lie down across the width of one end of the folded parachute. The rest of the children kneel down beside the child and help roll the child up in the parachute.

Adaptations

Place the folded parachute on top of mats on a low incline. Repeat the above steps, but have a child roll down the incline, wrapping up in the parachute while rolling.

Have a child sit or stand in the center of the parachute while the rest of the children walk around in a circle, slowly wrapping the child up with the parachute. Then slowly unwind in the opposite direction. Repeat the above step, but have two or more children in the center. (Refer to "Old Red Wagon" in the Sing-a-Long activity.)

Have one or two children wrap themselves up in the parachute. Whisper an animal name or an object name (such as "car") to the children hiding inside the parachute. The children inside move around in the parachute, imitating the animal or object sounds. The rest of the children try to guess what is being imitated.

Spread the parachute out fully on the floor and have some of the children lie down on the parachute side by side, with their feet facing the same direction. Wrap the parachute over the top of the children. Have the other children help you pull a large mat (a gymnastic mat works well) on top of the children covered with the parachute. If any of the children underneath are not covered by the mat, remove those children from the parachute. After checking to see that the children underneath are comfortable, assist the rest of the children to take turns rolling along the mat surface on top of the children underneath. Some children may need help rolling because it can be a bumpy road. The children inside the parachute really enjoy the weight of the mat and the children rolling over them. After everyone has had a turn rolling, have the children switch places. The children can also vary the way they move along the top of the mat (rolling forward or backward, doing somersaults, crawling).

Hot Dog

Spread the parachute out fully on the floor. Have the children roll the edges of the parachute into the center to make the shape of a hot-dog bun.

Have one child lie down in the bun and pretend to be the hot dog while the other children roll up the sides of the hot-dog bun.

The other children ask the "hot dog" what it wants on top: "Mustard?" "Relish?" "Onions?" The children pretend to sprinkle or spread ingredients on top of the hot dog.

Adaptations

Ask the children to decide how many of them should lie down to make the longest or shortest hot dog. (The children should all be lying in the same direction, feet pointing the same way.)

Ask the children to pretend to be other types of foods such as pizza, a sandwich, etc.

Monsters

Spread the parachute out fully and have all the children sitting, kneeling, or lying down on their stomachs or backs beneath the parachute.

Tell the children to remain very quiet and not to move at all. Then call out, "Is that you, Mr. Monster?" The children respond by moving their arms, legs, or other body parts underneath the parachute. The idea is for the children to listen for the direction and to interpret its meaning. For example, you may ask, "Mr. Monster, can you show me how big you are?" The children then interpret the meaning of "big." Some may stand up, others may lie on the floor and spread their arms and legs out wide, and others may work together to form one big group of children.

Adaptations

You may ask the children to stay underneath the parachute and try to move it around to different parts of the room. The children initially may need a little help figuring out this variation. You can help them pretend that they are little turtles and the parachute is their shell. The children can position themselves on their hands and knees with the parachute resting on their backs. As they move together, they carry the parachute around the room. The children in the front of the parachute must not go too fast or they will pull the parachute off the children in the back. This activity takes a lot of patience and teamwork.

Merry-Go-Round

Spread the parachute out fully and have the children sitting, kneeling, or standing around the parachute. Attach one colored marker or streamer to the outside edge of the parachute. This is the start point for the merry-go-round, and the child next to the streamer is responsible for noticing when the marker has returned to the start point. If you cannot attach a streamer, designate a child or one of the colored panels of the parachute to be the start point.

To play the game, the children pass the parachute to the left (or right, whichever direction you decide to start with first). When the parachute has returned to the start position, ask the children which way they want to move the parachute next (right or left).

Adaptations

When performing the following variations, the children who need physical help to move can be assisted by buddies, or they may choose to remain in one spot as the other children proceed around the parachute. If the parachute has handles around the outside, you can secure one of the loops to a wheelchair arm so the child can independently push or drive or be assisted to proceed around the circle without having to hold onto the parachute.

Have the children hold tightly onto the parachute and walk around first in one direction, then in the other. Have them try moving backwards, first clockwise, then counterclockwise.

As the children hold tightly onto the parachute with only one hand, they wave their free hands while they proceed around first in one direction, then the other. The children may also like to wave streamers or scarves with their free hands. If a child cannot hold onto the streamer or scarf, it can be attached to a wrist, an arm, a wheelchair, or crutches.

Spread the parachute out fully on the floor. Ask two or three children to get into the middle on top of the parachute. The other children pull the parachute taut and run around in one direction as fast as possible. The children in the middle can try to crawl against the turn, or they can just sit or lie still. If the children have good balance, they can even try walking on top of the parachute.

Jaws

Spread the parachute out fully and space the children evenly around the outside. The children can be sitting, kneeling, or standing. Designate one child to be "Jaws" and send this child underneath the parachute. The rest of the children hold tightly onto the parachute and move it up and down to make small waves. "Jaws" begins to move around underneath the parachute, crawling or pulling along on stomach or back. The children on the outside should not be able to see "Jaws" underneath.

"Jaws" touches the legs of a child who then screams and joins "Jaws" underneath the parachute. This child is now referred to as a "shark."

"Jaws" continues to touch other children until half of the children become "sharks" and are under the parachute. (Before "Jaws" begins, you may want to determine how many children need to be caught before you stop the game.) When "Jaws" reaches the predetermined number of children, stop the game, pick another child to be "Jaws," and start the game all over again.

Adaptations

You can signal to those holding the parachute to lift it up high. While the parachute is up, the "sharks" are free to escape to the outside. The last shark out becomes "Jaws," starting the game over again.

Parachute Throw

Spread the parachute out fully and space the children evenly around the outside. For this game, it is best to have the children sitting or standing. The children hold tightly onto the parachute and lift it up and down three times. On the third count (just as the parachute reaches its full height), have everyone let go. The parachute will float gracefully up and then down to the floor. It is very exciting to watch the parachute fly up in the air. (You may need to remind the children to stay in their places and not run after the parachute.)

Adaptations

Place a mat underneath the center of the parachute. Repeat the activity, but this time, after the children let go, have them quickly move onto the mat and wait to see if the parachute will land on top of them.

Have the children count as high as they can before letting go of the parachute (for example, lift it up and down 10 times, 15 times, and so on).

Magic Carpet

You will need at least two or three adults in addition to the children to perform this activity safely. Older children working together *may* be strong enough to lift another child inside the parachute, but be sure. Conduct this activity on a mat or a carpeted area.

Spread the parachute out fully on the floor and space the children evenly around the outside. Move together toward the center of the parachute as everyone gathers up the sides of the parachute, reducing the width as necessary to make a nest for a child to lie safely inside. The size of the nest will depend on the size of the child who is to be carried in the parachute. Generally, the size should equal the child's body length plus approximately two feet. If you are working with children under 5 years of age, one and a half feet may be plenty. If there is too much extra length, the children will have a difficult time lifting the parachute up off the floor.

The children work together to lower the parachute nest to the floor so a child can climb (or be assisted to lie down) inside. Check the location of the parachute's center hole. If it is in the center of the nest, have the children reroll the parachute so that the center hole is part of the rolled fabric and not part of the center, to prevent the child's head from slipping through it.

Have the children slowly and smoothly lift the magic carpet and child up off the ground. The child inside instructs the other children where to carry the parachute (to the door, a chair, and so on).

Adaptations

Try lifting the magic carpet off the ground, and experiment with slowly rocking it side to side, back and forth, or up and down.

Depending on the number of adults, as well as the children's ability to lift the parachute, one or more children can be positioned inside the parachute for a magic carpet ride.

Empty the Parachute

Spread the parachute out fully and space the children evenly around the outside. The children can be sitting, kneeling, or standing. Designate two or three children as "retrievers" and have the other children hold onto the parachute.

Place different sizes, shapes, and colors of balls, balloons, beach balls, or beanbags on top of the parachute.

Begin to move the parachute up and down to make small and large waves, trying to bounce the objects up and off the parachute.

As the objects fall off, the children designated as "retrievers" quickly pick up the objects and throw them back onto the parachute before it becomes emptied.

When the parachute is empty, the "retrievers" return to hold onto the parachute and another group of children takes a turn retrieving the objects and throwing them back onto the parachute.

Adaptations

The song "Popcorn" (described in the Sing-a-Long activity) can be sung with this game. Place small balls or beanbags on top of the parachute. When singing the first two phrases of the song, make small waves with the parachute. Begin to make bigger waves for the phrase, "sizzle, sizzle, sizzle, sizzle," but do not let the objects fall off. When you sing "pop," quickly lift the parachute up high, trying to bounce all the objects off the parachute.

Have the children who are retrieving the objects aim for the hole in the center as they throw the objects back onto the parachute. This is quite a challenging activity.

Ball Roll

Spread the parachute out fully and space the children evenly around the outside. The children should hold the parachute at waist level while sitting, kneeling, or standing.

Place a medium-sized gymnastic ball on top of the parachute. Holding onto the parachute edges, the group works together to move the ball out from the middle, coming as close as possible to the outside edge of the parachute. Once the ball is moved to this area, the goal is to coordinate the movement of the parachute up and down to move the ball around the outside as many times as possible. It takes practice and patience to find and maintain the right rhythm for moving the parachute. Part of the group needs to keep the parachute low while the rest of the group lift it up. This sequence is repeated all the way around the perimeter of the parachute. Lifting and lowering must be smooth and gradual to allow the ball to roll along. Moving too quickly will cause the ball to fall off.

Adaptations

Experiment with different types of balls (beach balls, sponge balls, balls with sound).

Try moving the balls in different directions—first to the right, then to the left, to the center, and back out to the edge.

Try to move the balls around the outside of the parachute, then toward the center to drop through the hole. You may wish to place a bucket or basket under the hole to catch the dropping balls.

Place a few children beneath the parachute to wait for the balls to drop down through the parachute's hole. The children pick the balls up and pass them back to the children on the perimeter.

Try changing the height where the parachute is held (shoulder, waist, knees, overhead), and repeat the above activities.

Play ball tag. Place two balls of different colors at opposite sides of the parachute. Decide which color will be "it" and whether it matters or not which direction the ball moves around the parachute. Have the children work the parachute up and down, trying to get the red ball to catch the blue ball. This is a very exciting game because the balls often come very close to each other but do not touch. Another variation of ball tag is to place a number of balls of two different colors on top of the parachute. The children try moving only the red balls around the outside while at the same time aiming the blue balls through the hole in the center of the parachute.

Mountain

Spread the parachute out fully and space the children evenly around the outside. The children lift the parachute up and down three times. Just as the parachute reaches its full height on the third count, the children quickly pull it down in front of them, placing their knees, feet, or wheelchair wheels on the top. The children have created a mountain or mushroom shape with the air trapped inside the parachute.

Have a few children leave their spots from around the parachute and try climbing up the mountain.

As more air is pushed out through the hole and from underneath the sides, the mountain or mushroom begins to collapse.

Adaptations

Slowly lower the parachute and continue to move the parachute up and down (wave action).

Have children who can use a wheelchair independently or with assistance move their wheelchairs over the top of the mountain and watch it flatten. Other children can also try walking over the top of the mountain, pushing air out as it is collapsing.

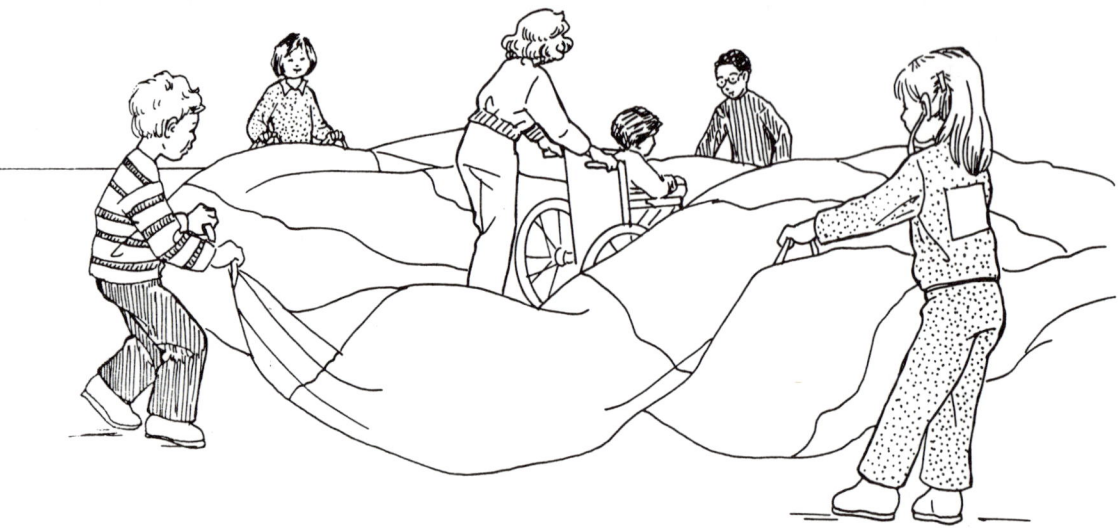

While some of the children secure the mountain, others can try rolling light-weight balls up and over the mountain or aim for the hole. Children on the other side need to watch for the balls that may come over.

Spaceship

Spread the parachute out fully and space the children evenly around the outside. Have the children hold on tight and lift and lower the parachute three times. On the count of three as the parachute reaches its full height, have the children move under it. The children lower themselves to the floor and, as they are sitting, they pull the parachute down behind their backs, securing it under their buttocks.

This creates an enclosed space. This is an excellent time for telling a story or singing a song (refer to Sing-a-Long). This is also a popular cool-down or closing activity.

If children in the group use wheelchairs or require physical assistance to sit, stand, or walk, the buddy system is recommended both when making the spaceship and in performing the spaceship activities. For the child in a wheelchair, the buddy should be positioned behind the wheelchair to help lower and secure the parachute behind and under the wheels. During the other variations, the buddy (with adult supervision) can assist the child into the center of the parachute under the hole and support the child in a comfortable position.

Adaptations

The children can rock the spaceship from side to side by pulling the parachute edges under their buttocks and gently leaning back, touching the parachute with their backsides. The children slowly begin to move their bodies from side to side, which causes the parachute to sway back and forth.

Prior to making the spaceship, you can place a few objects in the center beneath the parachute. Once the spaceship is formed, ask the children in turn to go to the center and pick up the object you named. Another variation using objects is to give the child specific cues (such as color, shape, or size) and have the child search for the correct one. Once children find the correct objects, they return to their places with the objects or rise up through the hole in the parachute and toss the objects out.

Children particularly enjoy coming up through the hole in the parachute, so you can try scattering objects on the floor outside of the parachute. Have the children take turns rising up through the hole to look for different objects. For example, ask a child to tell you the color of the ball. Is it big or small?

As the children lift the parachute up high, pick a child to let go of the parachute and go sit, kneel, or lie down directly under the hole. Have the rest of the children stand up and lift and lower the parachute over the child underneath. This variation should be done slowly and with your supervision. Some children enjoy raising their arms above their heads when they are underneath the parachute's hole.

Spread the parachute out fully on the floor. Have the children take turns crawling through the hole, disappearing underneath the parachute and into the "doghouse."

Repeat the steps to create a spaceship, but instead of having the children sit on the parachute, have them pull it down over their heads. The children can pretend they are wearing a hat. Children can perform this variation while standing, kneeling, or lying on their stomachs. When the children lie on the floor, their heads are under the parachute with the rest of their bodies outside.

Appendix
Common Childhood Conditions

This section provides general information about some of the childhood conditions that require special consideration. Each section gives a brief definition and points out some of the things you need to be aware of in working with children who have the condition. This information can help you to provide the most integrative experiences for the children in your groups. If you have specific concerns or questions regarding a child's condition or participation in physical activity, contact the child's primary caregivers. Additional information can be obtained from medical resources and from medical doctors and specialists. One or more references are listed for each condition, in case you want more information or need a place to start in researching the disorder.

Amputation

Amputation is the loss of a body part or parts resulting from a birth defect (congenital) or an accident (traumatic). A child may have one or more limbs affected. For any number of reasons, a child may not have an artificial limb (prosthesis), or the child may use different types of prostheses for different activities (sport limb versus conventional mechanical or myoelectric limb). Consult the primary caregivers and the child regarding wearing patterns. A child may find it more efficient not to wear the prosthesis for specific activities.

Special Considerations

Minimal adaptations are necessary for the child with an amputation to participate. However, a child wearing a lower-limb prosthesis may find balancing activities more difficult. A child wearing an upper-limb prosthesis may find coordinated arm movement activities more difficult.

Additional Information

Sherrill 1977, pp. 383-384

Wilcox and Peake 1988, p. 147

Arthritis

Arthritis is defined as inflammation of the joints. An affected joint may appear swollen, hot, red, and tender, with crepitation (cracking sounds when the joint is moved), and over time exhibit decreased range of motion, resulting in wasting of inactive muscles. There are three types of juvenile arthritis which are categorized according to their onset, number of joints involved, number of other body systems affected, and possibilities of recovery.

General Characteristics of Three Common Types of Arthritis

- pauci-articular: less than five joints usually affected (knee, ankle, elbow; less commonly, the finger and toe joints)
- polyarticular: may begin at any age, and affects girls more frequently. More than five joints are affected (knees, ankles, feet, wrists, hands, and neck)
- systemic: least common, but most serious. Begins before 5 years of age and affects both boys and girls. It involves other body systems. Acute periods may include high fevers, rashes, and enlargement of lymph nodes, liver, or spleen.

How Different Joints of the Body May Be Affected by Arthritis

Knee: swelling makes bending and straightening the leg difficult. The child may walk with a slight limp.

Ankle: lower leg muscles weaken and the Achilles tendon of the heel may become tight, resulting in a ducklike, flat-footed walk.

Feet: swelling makes footwear uncomfortable.

Wrist: decreased grip strength due to joint inflammation and muscle wasting. A later difficulty may be abnormal union of the bones (ankylosis).

Shoulder: increased difficulties moving the arm out to the side of the body (abduction), then lifting the arm overhead (flexion), or moving the arm behind (extension).

Elbow: swelling makes bending and straightening the forearm difficult.

Hip: increases difficulties moving (going up and down stairs, walking, sitting).

Special Considerations

If a child uses a wheelchair or any other piece of equipment (such as bracing), make sure that you are aware of its purpose and follow specific instructions for removing and positioning.

The child should be encouraged to participate during periods without inflammation (remission). Consult with primary caregivers and professionals as to whether the child is able to participate and in what activities.

Activities involving a lot of bending (flexion) of joints should be avoided, including:

- jumping activities (jumping rope, trampoline)
- activities in which falls may occur (rolling)
- contact sports
- horseback riding

Provide activities which promote slow extension of body parts.

Morning stiffness is common, and any prolonged periods of inactivity can result in stiffness. To relieve stiffness, have the child participate in a few minutes of general, slow body movements. Perform the following exercises with the child sitting or standing in a comfortable position:

- arms: moving up and down, back and forth, making large circles

- legs: moving leg back, extending knee, lifting toes up and down

Consult the child's primary caregiver or medical professional for additional stretching exercises.

Additional Information

Salter 1983, p. 191

Sherrill 1977, pp. 434-440

Asthma

Asthma is a lung condition characterized by spasms of the bronchial tubes, swelling of the linings, and increased release of mucus. These cause coughing, wheezing, difficult breathing, and a feeling of tightness in the chest. An asthma attack can last a few minutes or as long as several days. Since exercise may precipitate an acute attack, you should be familiar with the three stages through which an attack progresses: coughing, difficulty in breathing, and severe bronchial obstruction. For additional information, consult medical resources and/or contact a medical doctor.

Special Considerations

Although participation in vigorous activities may precipitate an acute attack, the child with a history of asthma should not be discouraged from participation. Rather, encourage participation within the child's limits to develop exercise tolerance.

When engaging in parachute activities, the child should be encouraged to use abdominal breathing techniques. This safeguards against overworking the upper chest muscles. During abdominal breathing, the child breathes air in (inhalation), the tummy protrudes, the diaphragm lowers, and the lungs expand. When the child breathes out (exhalation), the tummy flattens, the diaphragm relaxes and rises, and the lungs deflate as air is released.

Include rest breaks and periods of relaxation during specific parachute activities. Rest breaks not only provide physical rest but also control levels of excitement and safeguard against possible tightness in the chest.

Try to provide a total body exercise program, including the exercises below:

- forward and side bending (both in standing, kneeling, and sitting positions)
- arm raises and circles in backward directions
- blowing activities (such activities help reduce residual air in the lungs)
- blowing table-tennis balls or balloons across the parachute
- blowing out air underneath the parachute as it is raised
- abdominal muscle exercises (help to improve exhalation)

Additional Information

American National Red Cross 1977, p. 36

Sherrill 1977, pp. 350-368

Wilcox and Peake 1988, p. 147

Behavioral Disorders

It is important to discuss with the primary caregivers any known behavioral disorder. Listed below are characteristics which may or may not be found in a particular disorder.

General Characteristics of Behavioral Disorders

- impairment of emotional relationships
- preoccupation with inanimate objects
- loss or poor development of speech
- rocking, spinning behaviors (self-stimulating behaviors)
- resistance to change in the environment or routine
- unpredictable outbursts
- absence of a sense of personal identity
- intolerance of sensory stimuli (underactive or overactive response to tactile, auditory, or visual stimuli)
- may not exhibit affection and may not exhibit any awareness of others

Special Considerations

Provide a consistent and predictable approach to activities. If there is to be a change in the environment (such as playing with the parachute in another room or outside), prepare the child for this change ahead of time.

Remember that children who can talk may still refuse to talk or may refer to themselves in the third person.

Ensure that the environment is free of unnecessary equipment (such as extra chairs) which could be hazardous during an outburst.

Reward and reinforce appropriate, desirable behaviors and ignore inappropriate, undesirable behaviors. Consult with the primary caregivers and professionals working with the child to identify appropriate and inappropriate behaviors and specific ways to manage behaviors.

You may find that a child who normally relates more readily to inanimate objects may interact quite successfully with the parachute. In addition, children may improve their ability to maintain eye contact by watching the movement of the parachute as activities are performed.

Additional Information

Batshaw and Perret 1986, pp. 266-269

Cerebral Palsy

Cerebral palsy is a group of nonprogressive neuromuscular conditions caused by damage to different areas of the brain that control movement of the muscles. The damage may occur before, during, or after birth. The degree of motor involvement ranges from mild to severe and may also include associated impairments in hearing, vision, speech and language, and mental abilities.

Common Classifications to Describe Degree of Motor Involvement and Muscle Tone Patterns of Cerebral Palsy

Diplegia: primary involvement of the lower legs; may or may not involve upper limbs.

Hemiplegia: involvement of only one side of the body. Involvement may vary between arm and leg.

Triplegia: involvement of three limbs, usually both legs and one arm.

Quadriplegia: involvement of all four limbs.

Spastic: most common occurrence. As the child initiates movement (such as elbow flexion), the opposing muscles (elbow extensors) resist the pull. Limbs feel stiff to move (high tone). The child may also exhibit decreased tone (floppiness), especially in the trunk and facial muscles.

Athetoid: messages from the brain to the muscles are poorly coordinated. The motion is fast, involuntary, uncontrollable, and unpredictable.

Ataxia: least common occurrence. Ataxia refers to poor motor coordination. Usually the child exhibits unsteadiness of fine movements of the hands and an awkward walk.

Special Considerations

If a child uses a wheelchair or any other piece of equipment (such as bracing), make sure that you are aware of its purpose and follow specific instructions for removing and positioning.

When a child is using a wheelchair, it is important that the brakes are locked when it is not in motion. This is especially important whenever a child is transferring in or out of a wheelchair.

Do not forget that, while a wheelchair is a means of mobility, it may not be the only option for seating or mobility. Therefore, it is important to explore other positions (such as supported sitting positions). However, proper positions that are both comfortable and functional need to be reviewed with the primary caregivers and professionals (physical therapist, occupational therapist) responsible for the child's care.

Additional Information

Batshaw and Perret 1986, pp. 299-324

Connor, Williamson, and Siepp 1978

Finnie 1984

Cystic Fibrosis

Cystic fibrosis produces abnormal mucus secretion from the membranes of the internal organs. Two primary problems exist: the thick mucus clogs the bronchial tubes during breathing, and it plugs up the pancreatic ducts, reducing the release of digestive enzymes to the small intestine, which results in inadequate nutrition. Presently, there is no cure for cystic fibrosis. Instead, treatment involves prevention or control of lung infections, maintenance of proper nutrition, and prevention of salt loss. In order to manage cystic fibrosis, the child must undergo regular breathing exercises (daily aerosol therapy). Refer to medical resources and/or a medical doctor for additional information.

Special Considerations

If a child uses a wheelchair or any other piece of equipment (such as bracing), make sure that you are aware of its purpose and follow specific instructions for removing and positioning.

Additional Information

Sherrill 1977, p. 368

Diabetes

Diabetes is caused by insufficient levels of insulin in the bloodstream. Traditionally, diabetes has been classified into two types: juvenile (develops before 20 years of age) and adult onset. Individuals exhibiting juvenile diabetes are dependent upon insulin because the pancreas does not produce enough insulin. With adult onset diabetes, the pancreas is capable of manufacturing some insulin but the amount is inadequate. Such individuals usually can be treated with diet therapy and/or oral hypoglycemic drugs.

Special Considerations

Consult with the child's primary caregivers and/or medical professionals as to specific management needs.

A child with diabetes should be encouraged to participate in all activities. Over-exercise is not a problem; rather, the difficulty lies in the inability to judge ahead of time the amount of insulin needed.

Hearing Impairment

The degree of hearing impairment is measured in decibels. On the sound intensity scale, normal conversation measures 60 decibels (db). With a moderate hearing loss (40 to 60 db), normal conversation is interpreted as a whisper. Children with a profound hearing loss (80 to 100 db) are commonly referred to as "deaf." Both ears may not have the same degree of impairment, and only one ear may be affected. For additional information, consult medical resources and/or contact an audiologist.

Special Considerations

Find out what forms of communication the child is using: sign language, lip reading, speech, or any combinations. This information can be provided by primary caregivers, the child's speech-language pathologist, or the child's teacher.

Every effort must be made to make your speech clear. When you are speaking, make sure you face the child you are talking to and articulate your words clearly. This also provides the child with additional visual cues, such as facial expressions.

Decrease extraneous noises. Additional background noises not only interfere with the clarity of a speaker's speech, they can also be amplified if the child wears a hearing aid. Either situation results in a decrease in auditory discrimination.

At times a child with hearing impairments may experience balance difficulties. Note any problems in these areas.

Additional Information

American National Red Cross 1977, pp. 55-57

Wilcox and Peake 1988, p. 149

Learning Disabilities

Children with learning disabilities usually have average or above-average intelligence but may have difficulty interpreting and processing information which affects their abilities in one or more of the following areas: writing, reading, math, speech, social skills, gross and fine motor skills. Generally, children recognized as having learning disabilities are functioning at least two years below their peers in any one or more of the above areas.

General Characteristics of Learning Disabilities

- high level of activity (hyperactive); being in a constant state of motion
- underactive or overactive response to tactile, auditory, or visual stimuli
- decreased spatial awareness and/or depth perception
- short attention span, impulsivity
- easily fatigued
- gross and fine motor incoordination
- auditory language processing problems (appears to understand an instruction but responds differently)
- laterality and directionality difficulties
- exhibits extreme frustration
- poor social skills
- low self-esteem

Special Considerations

Break the activity down into smaller steps. This allows the child to achieve success and gain confidence.

A multisensory approach to learning is recommended (that is, incorporating visual, auditory, and physical mediums), but this needs to be monitored. A child may be hypersensitive to any one stimulus. You may find initially that certain parachute activities need to be avoided. However, as the child's confidence and tolerance of stimuli improve, additional activities should be incorporated.

Provide a combination of high- and low-energy activities, ending with a cool-down period. This not only relaxes the child but, more importantly, illustrates closure of an activity before initiating a new task.

To discourage children's impulsivity, ask them first to verbally describe what they are about to do. Another useful strategy is to have the child follow behind a slower child, waiting until the other child has taken a turn. If the child has finished taking a turn, assign another task (help someone else, help set up for the next activity). Remember that the assigned task must be purposeful. Merely keeping a child busy will not work. The child will quickly become aware of your strategy.

Simple visual cues can help a child who has difficulties following directions such as where to start, where to stop, and left/right. For example, post left and right arrows on walls or floor, or paint a circle on the floor.

Some children have no fear of danger. For example, a child may not realize that someone is under the parachute and may proceed to jump on top of the parachute. Clearly stating the rule of each activity helps prevent accidents.

Additional Information

Batshaw and Perret 1986, pp. 279-298

Sherrill 1977, pp. 296-308

Wilcox and Peake 1988, p. 150

Mental Retardation

The term "mental retardation" refers to significantly below-average mental ability associated with deficits in adaptive behavior. Mental retardation is usually apparent by early childhood, whether it begins at or before birth or occurs later in a child's development. In the past, it has been common to group children according to the severity of the mental deficits (mild/educable, moderate/trainable, severe/profound). However, there are great individual differences within these broad categories.

Many of the causes of mental retardation are known, but many are still unknown. For additional information, consult medical resources and/or contact a psychologist specializing in mental retardation.

Special Considerations

Use short, concise instructions.

Accompany verbal instructions with visual and physical demonstrations.

You may need to repeat directions. However, if you are constantly repeating directions, try simplifying your message or method of delivery. If difficulties still exist, contact the primary caregivers and professionals working with the child to review communication strategies.

Remember to observe each child's level of attention span. Lack of attention may be related to a number of factors which may include not understanding instructions or even boredom.

Encourage activities that require rhythmical repetition (for example, movement of the parachute up and down) and those that include large muscle groups and endurance.

Fear of new experiences may decrease the child's interest in the parachute. You can help the child to overcome this by first allowing time for observation of the activity, then working toward mastery of those skills with which the child feels comfortable.

Additional Information

Batshaw and Perret 1986, pp. 188-198

Sherrill 1977, pp. 459-488

Muscular Dystrophy

Muscular dystrophies are a group of genetically determined diseases characterized by progressive weakness and degeneration of muscle tissue. Onset is typically between the ages of 3 and 13 years. Boys are affected five to six times more frequently than girls. Generally, the child at later stages of the disease requires the use of a wheelchair (manual, then electric). Often the weakened respiratory and heart functions make the child more susceptible to other infections which may lead to a shortened life span. Although there are three common types of muscular dystrophies (Duchenne, Fascioscapularhumeral, and Juvenile), only Duchenne will be described because it affects more children. Refer to medical resources and/or a medical doctor for details of other muscular dystrophies.

General Characteristics of Duchenne Muscular Dystrophy

There are two types, the most common affecting only boys. The other type affects both boys and girls. Progression is less rapid although the characteristics are similar.

- onset before 3 up to 10 or 11 years
- awkward side-to-side, waddling walk
- difficulties running, riding a bike, climbing stairs
- frequent falls
- excessive forward tipping of the pelvis (lordosis)
- enlargement of muscles (hypertrophy). The fat and connective tissue that replace degenerating muscle fibers give a false impression of well-developed muscles when, in fact, the muscles are quite weak.

Special Considerations

If a child uses a wheelchair or any other piece of equipment (such as bracing), make sure that you are aware of its purpose and follow specific instructions for removing and positioning.

Exercise will not restore muscle power. It will, however, promote remaining strength and function of muscle tissues. Children should be encouraged to participate in physical activities to the best of their abilities. These children may fatigue earlier and require more frequent rest breaks.

Additional Information

Salter 1983, pp. 281-284

Sherrill 1977, pp. 422-426

Spina Bifida

Spina bifida is caused by failure of one or more sections of the neural tube around the spinal cord to close *in utero*. If surgery is necessary, it is usually performed soon after birth. Surgery attempts to close the openings of the spine to safeguard against infection. In some cases, a shunt may be placed in the brain to help drain off any excess fluid to relieve pressure on the brain.

General Characteristics of Three Common Types of Spina Bifida

Occulta: characterized by an abnormal hair growth, mole, dimple in the skin, or a split spinous process. Occulta usually causes no changes in posture and muscle tone. However, bladder or bowel control may be affected.

Meningocele: this condition is an outgrowth of the meninges (protective coverings) of the spinal cord. The spinal cord and nerve roots remain intact, but the meninges and the cerebrospinal fluid leak into the outgrowth (also referred to as the sac). Surgery is performed to remove the outgrowth. There may be mild paralysis (although uncommon), urinary or bowel incontinence, and loss of sensory awareness.

Myelomeningocele: outgrowth of the meninges which include both nerve endings and cerebrospinal fluid. Surgery is necessary. Depending on the spinal area involved, the child may experience partial to complete paralysis of the legs and trunk; associated urinary or bowel incontinence; and loss of touch, pain, and temperature sensation.

Special Considerations

In consultation with the primary caregivers and professionals working with the child, determine whether the child's ability to move body parts, associated urinary or bowel control, and touch, pain, or temperature sensation are affected.

If a child uses a wheelchair or any other piece of equipment (such as bracing), make sure that you are aware of its purpose and follow specific instructions for removing and positioning.

Because muscle contractions and deformities can occur due to muscle imbalances, ensure that the child is using appropriate sitting or standing positions. Consult with the primary caregivers and professionals for specifics.

Although it is not always apparent, a child with spina bifida may have difficulties with one or more of the following: visual and eye-hand coordination skills, receptive and expressive language skills (provide clear, concise, and concrete instructions), body awareness, and directionality (spatial concepts).

If a child needs assistance with urinary and bowel management, make sure that someone is trained in the proper procedures to reduce the frequency of accidents and that the child is comfortable with the person chosen to help.

Additional Information

    Batshaw and Perret 1986, p. 43

    Sherrill 1977, pp. 374-375

Visual Impairment

A person who is blind can see no more at a distance of 20 feet than a person with normal vision can see from 200 feet. Limited peripheral vision (20 degrees) is also classified as blind. Visual impairment also includes those who have sight of varying degrees. For additional information, consult medical resources and/or contact an ophthalmologist.

Special Considerations

Depending on the degree of visual impairment, the child may want to choose a friend to be a buddy. Make sure the buddy is shown how to hold out an arm to guide a visually impaired child. Encourage independence by ensuring that the buddy provides assistance only when necessary.

Use clear, concise instructions, giving descriptive verbal cues whenever possible. Make sure you describe any changes in routines. This will help the child be better prepared for the change.

You may wish to use fluorescent tape, colored paint, or textured materials to indicate a circle on the floor. This will not only assist a child with vision difficulty but will also remind the rest of the children where to stand.

When introducing a child to parachute activities, spread the parachute out fully and walk with the child around the outside to help the child gain an appreciation of its size. Then show the child where to hold onto the parachute.

Additional Information

Batshaw and Perret 1986, pp. 199-222

Wilcox and Peake 1988, p. 152

References

American National Red Cross. 1977. *Adapted aquatics: Swimming for persons with physical or mental impairments.* Garden City, NY: Doubleday and Company, Inc.

Batshaw, M. L., and Y. M. Perret. 1986. *Children with handicaps: A medical primer.* Baltimore, MD: Paul H. Brookes Publishing Co.

Connor, F. P., G. G. Williamson, and J. M. Siepp. 1978. *Program guide for infants and toddlers with neuromotor and developmental disabilities.* New York: Teachers College Press.

Finnie, N. R. 1984. *Handling the young cerebral palsied child at home.* London: William Heinemann Medical Books Ltd.

Kuntzleman, B., C. Kuntzleman, G. McGlynn, and M. McGlynn. 1982. *Aerobics with fun.* Spring Arbor, MI: Arbor Press.

Salter, R. B. 1983. *Textbook of disorders and injuries of the musculoskeletal system.* Baltimore, MD: Williams and Wilkins.

Sherrill, C. 1977. *Adapted physical education and recreation: A multidisciplinary approach.* Dubuque, IA: Wm. C. Brown Company Publishers.

Wilcox, C., and L. Peake. 1988. *Hey! What about me! Activities for disabled children.* Toronto: Doubleday Canada Limited.

Additional Sources

Adams, R. C., A. N. Daniel, and L. Pullman. 1972. *Games, sports, and exercises for the physically handicapped.* Philadelphia: Lea and Febiger.

American Occupational Therapy Association. 1986. *Play: A skill for life: Selected readings related to occupational therapy.* Rockville, MD.

American Psychiatric Association. 1987. *Diagnostic and statistical manual of mental disorders, III-R.* Washington, DC.

Anderson, D. R., G. D. Hodson, and W. G. Jones. 1975. *Instructional programming for the handicapped student.* Springfield, IL: Charles C. Thomas.

Bissel, J., J. Fisher, C. Owens, and P. Poleyn. 1988. *Sensory motor handbook: A guide for implementing and modifying activities in the classroom.* Torrance, CA: Sensory Integration International.

Burton, E. C. 1980. *Physical activities for the developing child.* Springfield, IL: Charles C. Thomas.

Campbell, W. 1988. *Fun around the parachute.* Pt. Claire, Quebec: Aquapercept.

Chaney, C., and N. Kephart. 1968. *Motoric aids to perceptual training.* Columbus, OH: Charles E. Merrill Publishing Co.

Cratty, B. J., and J. E. Breen. 1972. *Educational games for physically handicapped children.* Denver, CO: Love Publishing Company.

Dalley, M. L. 1983. *Moving and growing: Exercises and activities for the first two years.* Ottawa: Fitness Canada and Canadian Institute of Child Health.

Ellis, M. J. 1973. *Why people play.* Englewood Cliffs, NJ: Prentice Hall, Inc.

Espenschade, A. S., and H. M. Eckert. 1980. *Motor development.* Columbus, OH: Charles E. Merrill Publishing Co.

Evans, D. 1971. *Oh chute: Parachute activities for fun and fitness.* Sioux Falls, SD: Fun and Fitness.

Florey, L. 1971. An approach to play and play development. *American Journal of Occupational Therapy* 25:275-280.

Fluegelman, A., ed. 1976. *The new games book.* San Francisco: New Games Foundation.

Gallahue, D. L. 1982. *Developmental movement experiences for children.* Toronto: John Wiley and Sons.

_____. 1982. *Understanding motor development in children.* Toronto: John Wiley and Sons.

George, S., and B. Hart. 1983. *Physical education for handicapped children.* London: Souvenir Press.

Gilfoyle, E. M., A. P. Grady, and J. C. Moore. 1981. *Children adapt.* Thorofare, NJ: Charles B. Slack, Inc.

Hansen, J. (no date) *Moving and growing — Exercises and activities for 5's and 6's.* Ottawa: Fitness Canada.

Knickerbocker, B. 1980. *A holistic approach to the treatment of learning disorders.* Thorofare, NJ: Charles B. Slack, Inc.

Kogan, S. 1982. *Step by step: A complete movement education curriculum from preschool to sixth grade.* Byron, CA: Front Row Experiences.

Manolson, A. 1985. *It takes two to talk: A Hanen early language parent guide book.* Toronto: Hanen Early Language Resource Centre.

McClenaghan, B. A., and D. L. Gallahue. 1978. *Fundamental movement: A development and remedial approach.* Toronto: W. B. Saunders.

McInnes, J. M., and J. A. Treffry. 1982. *Deaf-blind infants and children.* Toronto, Ontario: University of Toronto Press.

Moghadam, H. 1988. *Attention deficit disorder: Hyperactivity revisited.* Calgary, Alberta: Detselig Enterprises Ltd.

Musselwhite, C. R. 1986. *Adaptive play for special needs children: Strategies to enhance communication and learning.* San Diego, CA: College-Hill Press.

Orlick, T. 1978. *The cooperative sports and games book.* New York: Pantheon Books.

Price, R. J. 1980. *Physical education and the physically handicapped child.* London: Lepus Books.

Reilly, M., ed. 1974. *Play as exploratory learning.* Beverly Hills, CA: Sage Publications.

Shepard, R. J. 1990. *Fitness in special populations.* Champaign, IL: Human Kinetics Books.

Simon, C. S. 1985. *Communication skills and classroom success.* San Diego, CA: College-Hill Press.

Stanford, D. J. 1982. *Guidelines for parents and teachers on play and play activity.* Dubuque, IA: Kendall Hunt Publishing Company.

Young, S. 1988. *Movement is fun.* Torrance, CA: Sensory Integration International.

More materials for sensorimotor therapy...

LEARNING ABOUT LEARNING DISABILITIES (VHS videotape)
by Judith Reisman, Ph.D., OTR, and Nancy Scott, B.S., OTR

Share valuable information on the sensory problems of learning disabilities in just 20 minutes! Watching this powerful video is both informative and touching. Use it for pre-service or in-service training with occupational and physical therapists, special educators, speech-language pathologists, teachers, and parents. See how the following sensory processing problems affect children—poor visual discrimination, poor auditory discrimination, auditory sensitivity, olfactory sensitivity, touch sensitivity, and coordination and movement problems

Catalog No. 4232-Y $69

SENSORY INTEGRATION THERAPY
by Toronto Sensory Integration Study Group

This 20-minute, full-color videotape allows you to explore the unique environment of sensory integration therapy. Use it to train therapists, students, teachers, or to educate parents. The program discusses the process of SI and shows characteristics and behaviors of children with SI disorders. It also outlines target areas for therapy. Plus, a balance of therapeutic activities provides the sensory motor foundation for learning.   **Catalog No. 4715-Y $69**

KELLIVEST™

Provide proprioceptive feedback with maximum calming deep pressure and help increase muscle tone with these weighted vests. Insert ½-, ¾-, or 1-pound weight pouches into the four interior pockets (two front, two back). Adjust the total vest weight to meet the needs of individual clients. The high positioning of the inner pockets assures the same calming deep pressure when either sitting or standing.

- Small (with 4 ½-lb. weights), Catalog No. 4246-Y $75
- Medium (with 4 ¾-lb. weights), Catalog No. 4247-Y $80
- Large (with 4 1-lb. weights), Catalog No. 4248-Y $85

Weight Pouches available for reorder in sets of 4—

- ½-lb., Catalog No. 4249-Y $12
- ¾-lb., Catalog No. 4250-Y $13
- 1-lb., Catalog No. 4251-Y $14

KELLIQUILT™

Provide proprioceptive feedback for clients who need quieting overall sensory input with this unique quilt. You'll have balanced, removable weight strips for adapting the quilt to clients of various ages and physical abilities. Use your quilt in conjunction with mat and swing exercises, as well as other activities in your therapy plan. Send it home with clients who have sleeping disorders or use in conjunction with your therapy exercises.

- Light (quilt with 5 3-lb. weights), Catalog No. 4252-Y $99
- Moderate (quilt with 5 4-lb. weights), Catalog No. 4253-Y $109
- Heavy (quilt with 5 5-lb. weights), Catalog No. 4254-Y $119

Therapy Skill Builders
A division of
Communication Skill Builders
3830 E. Bellevue/P.O. Box 42050
Tucson, Arizona 85733/(602) 323-7500